CCSS **Genre** Drama

W9-AWG-649

Essential Question
What can you discover when you give things a second look?

THE MYSTERIOUS TEACHER

by Feana Tu'akoi
illustrated by Andrew Burdan

Act 1
WHAT'S UP WITH MR. LIM?

Characters:

JACOB and **CALEB** (*brothers*)

VERA and **MIGUEL** (**JACOB** and **CALEB's** *friends*)

MR. LIM (**JACOB, VERA,** and **MIGUEL's** *teacher*)

OFFICER DAVIES (*local police officer*)

───────── **Scene 1** ─────────

Scene: *The classroom*

It's lunchtime, and **MR. LIM** *is sitting at his desk, concentrating on an open folder in front of him.* **JACOB, VERA,** *and* **MIGUEL** *enter.* **MR. LIM** *does not react.*

JACOB: Good afternoon, Mr. Lim!

MR. LIM: (*jumps up suddenly, slams the folder shut, and hides it behind his back*) Oh … ah, Jacob … Vera … Miguel … I didn't hear you come in.

VERA: Are you okay, Mr. Lim?

MR. LIM: (*clearing his throat*) I'm fine. What can I do for you kids?

MIGUEL: We want to ask about our science project.

JACOB: We're supposed to do our project in pairs, but Miguel doesn't have a partner.

VERA: (*studying* **MR. LIM**) So we wondered if he could work with us.

MR. LIM: That seems reasonable—as long as there's enough work for three people. What will your project be about?

MIGUEL: (*excitedly*) We're going to store popcorn kernels at different temperatures and see if that affects how well they pop.

JACOB: We're calling it "Popping Good Time!"

MIGUEL: (*grinning*) And we'll have a popping good time afterward when we eat all the great popcorn we've made!

frozen

cold

room temperature

warm

3

VERA: (*trying to see behind* **MR. LIM's** *back*) Mr. Lim, do you think storing them at different temperatures will make them taste different?

MR. LIM: (*moving so that* **VERA** *cannot see the folder*) That's another question you can try to answer with your project. Is there anything else?

JACOB: No, that's all.

VERA: (*looking concerned*) Are you okay, Mr. Lim?

MR. LIM: I'm fine, Vera. It's just not the best time, that's all. I have a lot on my plate at the moment.

VERA: Well, if you're sure …

MIGUEL: Come on, Vera. Let Mr. Lim finish his lunch in peace.

VERA: Okay. Good-bye, Mr. Lim.

VERA *takes one more look at* **MR. LIM,** *then follows* **MIGUEL** *and* **JACOB** *offstage.*

Scene: *The school playground at lunchtime*

JACOB, **MIGUEL**, *and* **VERA** *meet up with* **CALEB**. **CALEB** *has a mitt on his hand and is carrying a baseball.*

CALEB: Hey, guys. What's up?

JACOB: (*shrugging*) Not much.

MIGUEL: We've just been talking about our science project with Mr. Lim.

VERA: And, boy, was he acting weird!

CALEB: How do you mean?

VERA: Well, he couldn't wait for us to get out of there for starters.

MIGUEL: (*thinking about it*) Yeah, he did look kind of shocked when he first saw us walk in.

JACOB: Plus, he made sure we didn't see his folder.

CALEB: What folder?

VERA: He was looking at a folder when we came in. But as soon as he saw us, he quickly concealed it behind his back.

CALEB: That's weird.

MIGUEL: He seemed upset too.

JACOB *and* **VERA** *nod in agreement.*

CALEB: Upset?

MIGUEL: Angry, to be more precise. Maybe it's because we were in the classroom at lunchtime.

VERA: (*shaking her head*) I don't think he was angry. I think he was worried. He probably just received an upsetting letter from his grandparents in Korea.

JACOB: (*excitedly*) Or … maybe he's a spy working undercover for the U.S. government! He was probably looking at top-secret documents. No wonder he didn't want us to see!

CALEB: (*laughing at his brother*) A spy? I don't think so! Let's reconsider the facts. He's a teacher, and he has a folder that he doesn't want you to see. He must have been grading tests. Case solved!

JACOB: (*folding his arms and looking stubborn*) It was more than that, Caleb. Mr. Lim was definitely up to something.

VERA and **MIGUEL** *nod in agreement.*

CALEB: It's probably nothing, but let's follow him after school and see if he does anything suspicious.

MIGUEL: (*taking the baseball from* **CALEB**) And in the meantime, let's play ball. Come on, guys!

MIGUEL *leads the others offstage.*

STOP AND CHECK

What reasons do the children consider for Mr. Lim's odd behavior?

Act 2
TAILING THE TEACHER

Scene 1

Scene: *The sidewalk outside the school*

MR. LIM *is walking along the sidewalk with* **VERA, MIGUEL, JACOB,** *and* **CALEB** *not far behind. He does not know he is being followed. The kids crouch to one side of the stage at the front as* **OFFICER DAVIES** *comes in and shakes* **MR. LIM's** *hand.* **MR. LIM** *and* **OFFICER DAVIES** *move to the back of the stage and act out a conversation that the children cannot hear.*

VERA: What do you think they're talking about?

MIGUEL: I'm not sure, but Mr. Lim doesn't look very happy.

MR. LIM *shakes his head and looks at his feet.*

CALEB: That doesn't make any sense. Officer Davies is Mr. Lim's friend. Why would talking to him make Mr. Lim unhappy?

MIGUEL: Maybe he's in trouble.

JACOB: I told you he was up to something.

VERA: Look out—they're coming!

The children hide behind a bush as **MR. LIM** *and* **OFFICER DAVIES** *walk toward them.*

OFFICER DAVIES: I'd like you to come down to the police station tomorrow.

MR. LIM: (*shaking his head*) I can't do that.

OFFICER DAVIES: (*thinking for a moment*) Then you'll have to come with me now.

MR. LIM: (*sighing, then nodding slowly*) Yes, I guess you're right.

MR. LIM *follows* **OFFICER DAVIES** *offstage.*

MIGUEL: (*standing up from behind the bush*) What was all that about?

The others stand up, too.

CALEB: (*shaking his head in confusion*) I don't know, but I sure want to find out.

JACOB: Me too.

VERA: (*grinning*) Let's go stake out the police station!

VERA *leads the way offstage.*

Scene 2

Scene: *Outside the local police station*

JACOB *and* **CALEB** *sit on a bench, and* **VERA** *and* **MIGUEL** *stand next to them.*

JACOB: (*excitedly*) I told you Mr. Lim is a spy! He's in there sharing information with the police right now!

VERA: (*shaking her head*) I don't think so. He's just had bad news from Korea, and he's asking if the police can help. That's why he was so unhappy when he was talking to Officer Davies.

MIGUEL: I think he has to pay for some tickets—maybe for parking or speeding. That's why he was upset when we came into the classroom. He didn't want to look bad in front of us. Poor Officer Davies—imagine having to arrest your friend!

CALEB: (*laughing and shaking his head*) I'm astounded at you three! You have way too much imagination! Mr. Lim and Officer Davies are friends. Mr. Lim doesn't have time to see him tomorrow, so he's made time today, even though he's busy. Case closed!

JACOB: (*pointing offstage*) Maybe we should ask him. Here he comes now.

MR. LIM *enters, sees the group, and looks flustered.*

MR. LIM: Oh … ah … hello, everybody.

VERA: Everything okay, Mr. Lim? You don't seem like yourself.

MR. LIM: Seeing you all has perplexed me, but I'm fine. Really.

MIGUEL: Mr. Lim, is there something going on? You can tell us.

MR. LIM: (*in a sharp tone and frowning*) You'll find out soon enough. I have to go now.

> **MR. LIM** *exits.*

CALEB: That's weird. Mr. Lim never snaps. How should we interpret that?

JACOB: (*smiling knowingly*) It's the stress from having a secret identity. Spies don't like to be followed.

STOP AND CHECK

Why are the children following Mr. Lim?

Act 3
MYSTERY SOLVED!

Scene: *The next afternoon in the school classroom*

MR. LIM *is standing at the front of the class, yawning and rubbing his eyes.* **JACOB**, **VERA**, *and* **MIGUEL** *sit chatting at their desks.*

VERA: Mr. Lim looks as though he didn't sleep last night. He must be worried about his grandparents.

MIGUEL: (*shaking his head*) No, he's worried about how to pay his parking tickets.

JACOB: Wrong! His cover has been blown. It's the worst thing that can happen to a spy.

VERA *and* **MIGUEL** *shake their heads and grin.*

MR. LIM: May I have everyone's attention, please?

Everyone settles down and stops talking.

MR. LIM: I have something important to tell you.

13

VERA *grins and looks at* **MIGUEL**.

VERA: This is it! Pay attention.

The children sit up straight and lean forward to listen.

MR. LIM: (*looking pointedly at* **VERA**, **MIGUEL**, *and then* **JACOB**) As some of our more inquisitive class members know, I took a trip to the police station yesterday afternoon. I didn't want to tell anyone until I was absolutely certain, but last night, I received the go-ahead for a field trip to the old town jail.

MIGUEL: (*shocked*) The old town jail? But that's been closed for years. No one's allowed there without special permission.

MR. LIM: (*grinning*) That's right. My friend Officer Davies has organized it for us. We're going to have a full tour—we can even go into the empty cells!

The children start chatting excitedly to one another.

VERA: Everything makes sense now. We all got it wrong.

JACOB: (*grinning*) Not me. I still think he's a spy.

MIGUEL *rolls his eyes and shakes his head.*

MR. LIM: (*holding his hands up for quiet*) This field trip will be great for our unit on local history. It will give us a real feel for how things used to be in this town. Experience is the best teacher.

MIGUEL: (*raising his hand*) Sounds good, Mr. Lim. When are we going?

MR. LIM: Next week. I was up late last night doing all the paperwork. Now it's your turn. (*handing out permission slips*) Take these permission slips home and have them signed. No permission slip, no trip.

VERA: (*taking her permission slip and turning to* **JACOB** *and* **MIGUEL**) This field trip sounds amazing. I can't wait to tell my mom!

JACOB: (*grinning*) I can't wait to tell Caleb. Case closed!

MIGUEL, JACOB, *and* **VERA** *high-five one another and exit.*

> **STOP AND CHECK**
>
> Why had Mr. Lim been acting so strangely?

Respond to Reading

Summarize

Use important details from *The Mysterious Teacher* to summarize what the characters discovered and how. Your graphic organizer may help you.

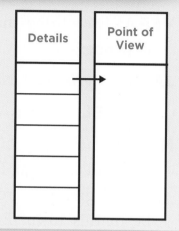

Details	Point of View

Text Evidence

1. What three features of the text show you it is a drama? **GENRE**

2. In Act 1, Scene 2, what is Caleb's point of view about Mr. Lim? What does he say that expresses this point of view? **POINT OF VIEW**

3. What does the expression "experience is the best teacher" mean on page 15? What clues help you figure it out? **ADAGES**

4. Write about how Mr. Lim's role as a teacher who is planning a surprise affects how he speaks and acts. Include examples from the dialogue and stage directions. **WRITE ABOUT READING**

Compare Texts

Read a story about the way a boy took another look to make a discovery.

The Case of the Missing Nectarine

"Hey! There's a nectarine missing," exclaimed Dad as he busily prepared lunches for the entire family. "I only bought them yesterday, and I warned everyone that they were going in our lunches today. So who's the culprit?"

Mom peered up from behind her newspaper. "It wasn't me, as much as I love juicy nectarines."

"Don't look at me, Dad. I haven't been in the kitchen," said Sarah, texting on her phone.

"There's definitely one missing—I know that I bought four so that we'd each have one for lunch, but now there are only three," explained Dad. He let out an exasperated sigh.

"Well, Sarah and I didn't eat it," stressed Mom. "How about you, Josh?"

Josh looked up from his detective novel. "Not guilty," he replied solemnly.

Illustration: Scott Pearson

Dad frowned and crossed his arms. "Somebody took it. Be honest and own up," he prodded.

Josh jumped up and placed his novel on the floor. "Don't panic, Dad. I've read loads of detective books, so I know just what to do."

Sarah rolled her eyes and let out a loud sigh.

Josh ignored her. "First, we need to determine if there really is a crime to investigate. Hand me the supermarket receipt, please, Dad."

Dad looked at Josh strangely, but he reached into his wallet and handed over the receipt. Josh got the scale out of the kitchen cupboard, carefully weighed the nectarines, and then confirmed the weight on the receipt.

"You're correct," he told Dad. "One's missing."

He emptied out the fruit bowl and investigated the fridge, but there was no sign of the missing nectarine.

Next, he made a suspect list of all the family members and asked everyone where they had been when Dad came home with the groceries and unloaded them in the kitchen.

Mom and Sarah reminded him that they had been at swim practice, so that ruled them out.

Then, Josh remembered something he had observed. "I saw you eating something when you were putting the groceries away, and you love nectarines!" he accused Dad.

Dad looked extremely embarrassed. "It wasn't a nectarine that I was eating, Josh," he said sheepishly. "It was the last piece of Mom's chocolate mud cake—I couldn't resist."

"Hmmm, this case is a lot tougher than I expected," said Josh. "We need a reenactment. Pick up the shopping bag, Dad, and show us exactly what you did when you got home."

Dad felt silly, but he reached for the bag anyway. That was when Josh noticed the bulge at the bottom. "Case solved!" he cried, pointing. "The nectarine is still in the shopping bag. Am I a great detective, or what?"

For once, Sarah did not utter a word.

Make Connections

What did Josh do to solve the mystery in *The Case of the Missing Nectarine*? **ESSENTIAL QUESTION**

What did the characters in each of the stories have to do to discover the truth about the mysteries? **TEXT TO TEXT**

Illustration: Scott Pearson

Focus on
Literary Elements

Foreshadowing Writers of stories or dramas with a mystery often give hints or clues about what is to come later in the story. This is called foreshadowing. Like a shadow that stretches out in front of you when the sun is behind you, the clues in a story can be seen before the real outcome is revealed.

Read and Find The children in *The Mysterious Teacher* notice that their teacher is behaving strangely because the author shows him doing and saying mysterious things. These are the hints that lead the children to follow Mr. Lim and suggest reasons for his behavior. Look for the clue on page 2. What was the author foreshadowing? What did you think Mr. Lim might be up to?

Your Turn

Read Act 2 of *The Mysterious Teacher* aloud in your group as readers' theater. Some people might need to read two parts. Read Mr. Lim's lines in a way that will make his seemingly suspicious behavior (the foreshadowing) clear to an audience. How does his behavior and the tone of his lines change in Act 3?